I CAN BE A
REPORTER

By Christine Maloney Fitz-Gerald

Prepared under the direction of Robert Hillerich, Ph.D.

CHILDRENS PRESS ®

CHICAGO

Fitz-Gerald, Christine Maloney.
  I can be a reporter.
  (I can be)
  Summary: Discusses the work reporters do in gathering
material for stories and then writing them.
  1. Reporters and reporting—Vocational guidance—
Juvenile literature. [1. Reporters and reporting—
Vocational guidance. 2. Vocational guidance.
3. Occupations] I. Title. II. Series.
PN4776.F5 1986   070.4'3'023   86-9614
ISBN 0-516-01899-X

PICTURE DICTIONARY

tape recorder

reporter

notes

beat

on the scene

deadline

headline

editorial

Above: A reporter might write a story about a new baby or a neighborhood fire. Below: Like this man telling stories in a park, all good storytellers know how to capture your attention.

Everyday events can
make exciting stories.
Do you tell good stories
about things that
happen in your school
and neighborhood—
parties, street repairs,
new babies, thunderstorms?
Are you curious about
why and how things
happen? Then you may
have a "nose for news."
All good reporters need that.

reporter

Wherever there's a crowd, reporters know there's something people will want to read about.

Reporters are always
alert for a "lead," a
clue that points the way
to a story. They know
that good stories are
everywhere, waiting to
be found. A talk with

A museum's new totem pole (left) and a baby zebra born to a horse (right) make good story subjects for a reporter.

an animal trainer, a new downtown building, a baseball game, a new traffic law, a very hot summer—a reporter might turn any of these into a good story.

Reporters check their facts (left) and interview
people (right) to make sure everything they write is true.

Reporters write true
stories and make them
interesting to read. They
gather facts by talking
to people and reading.
They spend a lot of
time on this part of the
job because their
stories must be true.

Reporters often use tape recorders so they can report a person's exact words. Some tape recorders hook up to a telephone (left). Some are hand-held (right) to record a speaker in person.

They write notes on the facts they find out. Sometimes they use tape recorders to make sure they report what someone says correctly.

notes

tape recorder

Once a reporter has all of the facts, it's time to write. The writing must be lively because no one will read a dull story. Reporters try to write a story that will grab readers' attention and make them want to read the story.

To meet deadlines, reporters may have to talk to people about their stories and write at the same time.

All reporters have a deadline, or a time by which their stories must be finished. Since most reporters work for newspapers that are printed daily, they work quickly. A story is "news"

deadline

for a very short time. Newspapers don't want stale old stories. They need fresh stories about things that happened that very day. So it's not odd for a reporter to find, research, and write a story all in one day.

Magazine, TV, and radio station reporters work with deadlines,

TV reporters interview a skier (left) and a race car driver (right) on the spot. Sports fans who are watching want to know what sports stars are feeling and thinking when they compete.

too. The reporters you see on TV are sometimes reporting "live," making up their story on the spot.

How do reporters find stories to write?

Some have a "beat"—a place they visit regularly to look for stories. The beat could be the town hall or the police station. Reporters spend a lot of time on the beat because they must cover any story that happens there.

beat

Left: Reporter getting a policeman's story. Right: Sports reporter writing about a baseball game on a portable computer. The computer sends the story to the newspaper office through the telephone.

Other reporters write
stories on a subject they
know a lot about. It
could be anything—
baseball, fashion,
money, buildings, art,
travel, food. Their

articles may tell people which cars are good buys, how to save money, or which restaurants have good food. It's easy to think of good stories about something you like.

Some reporters write stories to tell what they think about some big issue. Who should be president and why?

Reporters at a press conference in Washington, D.C. Some of these reporters may write editorials about what they find out here.

How can we raise
money to repair roads?
Stories that give the
newspaper publisher's
opinion are called
editorials. It may sound

editorial

easy to write an editorial, but it's really difficult. People write their editorials carefully because they may change the way their readers feel about things.

Big city newspapers ask their reporters to find good stories and write them. Small town newspapers may ask their reporters to do other things as well.

Writing headlines (left) is a special skill. The headline must tell what a story is about in a few words. Each page must be laid out (right) so that it will attract the readers' attention.

Their reporters may photograph events and write headlines or titles for stories. They may even help to lay out the paper, deciding which article goes on which

headline

19

Above: Reporters get to meet interesting people like an architect (left) or the owner of a fancy car (right). Below: Reporters enable *us* to meet famous people, too, like Chicago Cub Keith Moreland (left) and clothing designer Calvin Klein (right).

page and which stories should have photos.

Reporting the news is exciting. Reporters meet interesting people and see some wonderful things. Often they travel on the job. They enjoy reading their stories in the paper, seeing them on TV, or hearing them on the radio.

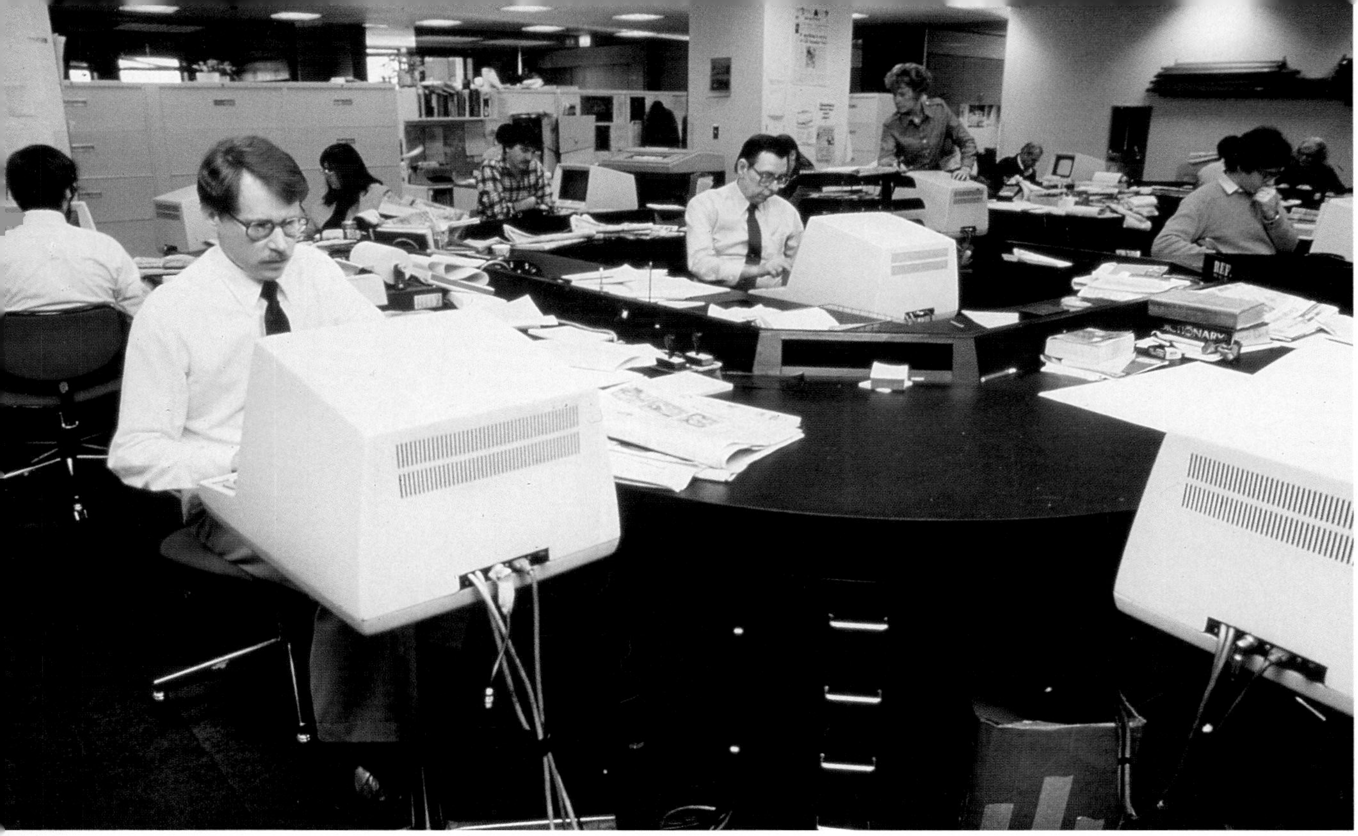

Reporters work late into the night so we can read the latest news in the morning.

But the job is not easy. News can happen any time, so some reporters work all night just so their newspaper doesn't miss a big story. Working quickly to meet deadlines is hard work.

A TV cameraman getting a bird's-eye view for a reporter down on the ground

Some reporting jobs are dangerous. It's interesting to read about a faraway volcano or earthquake, but a reporter has to be right there on the scene to get the facts.

on the scene

Wherever news is happening, a reporter is there. The news may be a fire (top), a volcano (left), or an event at Kennedy Space Center (above).

Plan on going to college if you want to be a reporter. Most reporters study journalism for four years. They also type well.

Learn as much as you can about other things that interest you. You could specialize in writing about a favorite subject.

It is important to learn to write and type well if you want to be a reporter.

Practice writing. Reporters need to write well. But above all, they must write the truth because people believe their stories.

Wouldn't you like *your* stories to reach thousands of people every day?

If something interests you and you can think of a good story about it, your story will interest other people, too. As a reporter, you could write the newspaper, magazine, TV, and radio stories that people read and hear every day.

WORDS YOU SHOULD KNOW

article (ARE • tih • kul)—a story about a news event or a particular subject in a newspaper or magazine

beat (BEET)—a place that a reporter visits regularly to look for something to write about

deadline (DED • line)—the time by which a reporter must finish a story and turn it in

editorial (ed • ih • TOH • ree • ul)—an article that tells what the writer thinks about an important subject

headline (HED • line)—the title of a newspaper story

issue (ISH • oo)—a question or subject on which people have differing opinions

journalism (JER • nul • izm)—the study of news writing for newspapers and magazines

lead (LEED)—a clue that may point the way to a good story

live (LYV)—something that appears on TV or radio at the same time that it is happening

opinion (oh • PIN • yun)—what someone thinks about a subject

research (REE • surch)—to find out facts about a subject by reading or asking questions about it

specialize (SPEH • shul • ize)—to concentrate on one particular subject or area

INDEX

PHOTO CREDITS

ABOUT THE AUTHOR

Christine Fitz-Gerald has a B.A. in English Literature from Ohio University and a Masters in Management from Northwestern University. She has been employed by the Quaker Oats Co. and by General Mills. Most recently, she was a strategic planner for a division of Honeywell, Inc. in Minneapolis. She now resides in Chicago with her husband and two young children.